WHO NEEDS TO KNOW

By TL Bliss

Printed in the United States of America

Cover Design: TL Bliss

Written and Prepared By: TL Bliss

Published By: TL Bliss

First Edition, 2016

ABOUT THE AUTHOR

"I started writing poems when I was just a little girl. I never did much with anything I had written other than read it a few times and then put it away. Over the years, everything I had written was lost or destroyed, but the memories I had still lingered on in my mind. We all struggle with things deep within us and outside of us that intrigues our senses enough to want to tell the world about it; why not share what stimulates us and sparks our emotions through a book." ~~TL Bliss

Visit www.tlbliss.com for more information and links to purchase other stories written by TL Bliss.

"On March 23, 2016, my biological father passed away. In the meantime, our torn and tattered family had all gone their own separate ways earlier in life; neither knowing where the other was nor having any contact information. This book was prepared with that single thought in mind. Keep track of your contacts and their information all in one location. There should never be a struggle when it comes to contacting family and friends in your time of need." ~~TL Bliss

TL Bliss

This page has been left blank intentionally

MY CONTACT INFORMATION:

MY CONTACT INFORMATION:

First Name:_____

Last Name: _____

Maiden Name: _____

Date of Birth: _____

Home Address: _____

Home Phone: _____

Cell Phone: _____

Work Phone: _____

Email Address: _____

Notes: _____

_____

_____

_____

_____

_____

_____

_____

_____

_____

_____

_____

IN CASE OF EMERGENCY, CONTACT:

First Name:_____

Last Name: _____

Maiden Name: _____

Date of Birth: _____

Home Address: _____

Home Phone: _____

Cell Phone: _____

Work Phone: _____

Email Address: _____

Notes: _____

_____

_____

_____

_____

_____

MY CONTACT INFORMATION:

First Name:_____

Last Name: _____

Maiden Name: _____

Date of Birth: _____

Home Address: _____

Home Phone: _____

Cell Phone: _____

Work Phone: _____

Email Address: _____

Notes: _____
_____
_____
_____
_____
_____
_____
_____
_____
_____
_____
_____
_____
_____

IN CASE OF EMERGENCY, CONTACT:

First Name:_____

Last Name: _____

Maiden Name: _____

Date of Birth: _____

Home Address: _____

Home Phone: _____

Cell Phone: _____

Work Phone: _____

Email Address: _____

Notes: _____
_____
_____
_____
_____
_____

MY CHILDREN

MY CHILDREN

First Name:_____

Last Name: _____

Maiden Name: _____

Date of Birth: _____

Home Address: _____

Home Phone: _____

Cell Phone: _____

Work Phone: _____

Email Address: _____

Notes: _____

_____

_____

_____

_____

_____

_____

_____

_____

First Name:_____

Last Name: _____

Maiden Name: _____

Date of Birth: _____

Home Address: _____

Home Phone: _____

Cell Phone: _____

Work Phone: _____

Email Address: _____

Notes: _____

_____

_____

_____

_____

_____

_____

_____

MY CHILDREN

First Name:_____
Last Name: _____
Maiden Name: _____
Date of Birth: _____
Home Address: _____
Home Phone: _____
Cell Phone: _____
Work Phone: _____
Email Address: _____

Notes: _____
_____
_____
_____
_____
_____
_____
_____
_____
_____
_____

First Name:_____
Last Name: _____
Maiden Name: _____
Date of Birth: _____
Home Address: _____
Home Phone: _____
Cell Phone: _____
Work Phone: _____
Email Address: _____

Notes: _____
_____
_____
_____
_____
_____
_____
_____
_____

MY CHILDREN

First Name:_____

Last Name: _____

Maiden Name: _____

Date of Birth: _____

Home Address: _____

Home Phone: _____

Cell Phone: _____

Work Phone: _____

Email Address: _____

Notes: _____

_____

_____

_____

_____

_____

_____

_____

_____

_____

First Name:_____

Last Name: _____

Maiden Name: _____

Date of Birth: _____

Home Address: _____

Home Phone: _____

Cell Phone: _____

Work Phone: _____

Email Address: _____

Notes: _____

_____

_____

_____

_____

_____

_____

_____

_____

MY CHILDREN

First Name:_____

Last Name: _____

Maiden Name: _____

Date of Birth: _____

Home Address: _____

Home Phone: _____

Cell Phone: _____

Work Phone: _____

Email Address: _____

Notes: _____

_____

_____

_____

_____

_____

_____

_____

_____

_____

First Name:_____

Last Name: _____

Maiden Name: _____

Date of Birth: _____

Home Address: _____

Home Phone: _____

Cell Phone: _____

Work Phone: _____

Email Address: _____

Notes: _____

_____

_____

_____

_____

_____

_____

_____

_____

MY CHILDREN

First Name:_____
Last Name: _____
Maiden Name: _____
Date of Birth: _____
Home Address: _____
Home Phone: _____
Cell Phone: _____
Work Phone: _____
Email Address: _____

Notes: _____
_____
_____
_____
_____
_____
_____
_____
_____
_____
_____

First Name:_____
Last Name: _____
Maiden Name: _____
Date of Birth: _____
Home Address: _____
Home Phone: _____
Cell Phone: _____
Work Phone: _____
Email Address: _____

Notes: _____
_____
_____
_____
_____
_____
_____
_____
_____
_____

ADDITIONAL FAMILY

ADDITIONAL FAMILY

First Name:_____

Last Name: _____

Maiden Name: _____

Date of Birth: _____

Home Address: _____

Home Phone: _____

Cell Phone: _____

Work Phone: _____

Email Address: _____

Notes: _____
_____
_____
_____
_____
_____
_____
_____
_____
_____
_____

First Name:_____

Last Name: _____

Maiden Name: _____

Date of Birth: _____

Home Address: _____

Home Phone: _____

Cell Phone: _____

Work Phone: _____

Email Address: _____

Notes: _____
_____
_____
_____
_____
_____
_____
_____
_____

ADDITIONAL FAMILY

First Name:_____

Last Name: _____

Maiden Name: _____

Date of Birth: _____

Home Address: _____

Home Phone: _____

Cell Phone: _____

Work Phone: _____

Email Address: _____

Notes: _____
_____
_____
_____
_____
_____
_____
_____
_____
_____
_____

First Name:_____

Last Name: _____

Maiden Name: _____

Date of Birth: _____

Home Address: _____

Home Phone: _____

Cell Phone: _____

Work Phone: _____

Email Address: _____

Notes: _____
_____
_____
_____
_____
_____
_____
_____
_____
_____

ADDITIONAL FAMILY

First Name:_____
Last Name: _____
Maiden Name: _____
Date of Birth: _____
Home Address: _____
Home Phone: _____
Cell Phone: _____
Work Phone: _____
Email Address: _____

Notes: _____
_____
_____
_____
_____
_____
_____
_____
_____
_____
_____

First Name:_____
Last Name: _____
Maiden Name: _____
Date of Birth: _____
Home Address: _____
Home Phone: _____
Cell Phone: _____
Work Phone: _____
Email Address: _____

Notes: _____
_____
_____
_____
_____
_____
_____
_____
_____

ADDITIONAL FAMILY

First Name:_____

Last Name: _____

Maiden Name: _____

Date of Birth: _____

Home Address: _____

Home Phone: _____

Cell Phone: _____

Work Phone: _____

Email Address: _____

Notes: _____
_____
_____
_____
_____
_____
_____
_____
_____
_____
_____

First Name:_____

Last Name: _____

Maiden Name: _____

Date of Birth: _____

Home Address: _____

Home Phone: _____

Cell Phone: _____

Work Phone: _____

Email Address: _____

Notes: _____
_____
_____
_____
_____
_____
_____
_____
_____

ADDITIONAL FAMILY

First Name:_____

Last Name: _____

Maiden Name: _____

Date of Birth: _____

Home Address: _____

Home Phone: _____

Cell Phone: _____

Work Phone: _____

Email Address: _____

Notes: _____
_____
_____
_____
_____
_____
_____
_____
_____
_____
_____

First Name:_____

Last Name: _____

Maiden Name: _____

Date of Birth: _____

Home Address: _____

Home Phone: _____

Cell Phone: _____

Work Phone: _____

Email Address: _____

Notes: _____
_____
_____
_____
_____
_____
_____
_____
_____
_____

ADDITIONAL FAMILY

First Name:_____

Last Name: _____

Maiden Name: _____

Date of Birth: _____

Home Address: _____

Home Phone: _____

Cell Phone: _____

Work Phone: _____

Email Address: _____

Notes: _____
_____
_____
_____
_____
_____
_____
_____
_____
_____
_____

First Name:_____

Last Name: _____

Maiden Name: _____

Date of Birth: _____

Home Address: _____

Home Phone: _____

Cell Phone: _____

Work Phone: _____

Email Address: _____

Notes: _____
_____
_____
_____
_____
_____
_____
_____
_____
_____

ADDITIONAL FAMILY

First Name:_____

Last Name: _____

Maiden Name: _____

Date of Birth: _____

Home Address: _____

Home Phone: _____

Cell Phone: _____

Work Phone: _____

Email Address: _____

Notes: _____
_____
_____
_____
_____
_____
_____
_____
_____
_____
_____

First Name:_____

Last Name: _____

Maiden Name: _____

Date of Birth: _____

Home Address: _____

Home Phone: _____

Cell Phone: _____

Work Phone: _____

Email Address: _____

Notes: _____
_____
_____
_____
_____
_____
_____
_____
_____
_____

ADDITIONAL FAMILY

First Name:_____

Last Name: _____

Maiden Name: _____

Date of Birth: _____

Home Address: _____

Home Phone: _____

Cell Phone: _____

Work Phone: _____

Email Address: _____

Notes: _____
_____
_____
_____
_____
_____
_____
_____
_____
_____

First Name:_____

Last Name: _____

Maiden Name: _____

Date of Birth: _____

Home Address: _____

Home Phone: _____

Cell Phone: _____

Work Phone: _____

Email Address: _____

Notes: _____
_____
_____
_____
_____
_____
_____
_____
_____

ADDITIONAL FAMILY

First Name:_____

Last Name: _____

Maiden Name: _____

Date of Birth: _____

Home Address: _____

Home Phone: _____

Cell Phone: _____

Work Phone: _____

Email Address: _____

Notes: _____
_____
_____
_____
_____
_____
_____
_____
_____
_____
_____

First Name:_____

Last Name: _____

Maiden Name: _____

Date of Birth: _____

Home Address: _____

Home Phone: _____

Cell Phone: _____

Work Phone: _____

Email Address: _____

Notes: _____
_____
_____
_____
_____
_____
_____
_____
_____

ADDITIONAL FAMILY

First Name:_____
Last Name: _____
Maiden Name: _____
Date of Birth: _____
Home Address: _____
Home Phone: _____
Cell Phone: _____
Work Phone: _____
Email Address: _____

Notes: _____
_____
_____
_____
_____
_____
_____
_____
_____
_____
_____

First Name:_____
Last Name: _____
Maiden Name: _____
Date of Birth: _____
Home Address: _____
Home Phone: _____
Cell Phone: _____
Work Phone: _____
Email Address: _____

Notes: _____
_____
_____
_____
_____
_____
_____
_____
_____

ADDITIONAL FAMILY

First Name:_____

Last Name: _____

Maiden Name: _____

Date of Birth: _____

Home Address: _____

Home Phone: _____

Cell Phone: _____

Work Phone: _____

Email Address: _____

Notes: _____
_____
_____
_____
_____
_____
_____
_____
_____
_____
_____

First Name:_____

Last Name: _____

Maiden Name: _____

Date of Birth: _____

Home Address: _____

Home Phone: _____

Cell Phone: _____

Work Phone: _____

Email Address: _____

Notes: _____
_____
_____
_____
_____
_____
_____
_____
_____
_____

ADDITIONAL FAMILY

First Name:_____

Last Name: _____

Maiden Name: _____

Date of Birth: _____

Home Address: _____

Home Phone: _____

Cell Phone: _____

Work Phone: _____

Email Address: _____

Notes: _____

_____

_____

_____

_____

_____

_____

_____

_____

_____

First Name:_____

Last Name: _____

Maiden Name: _____

Date of Birth: _____

Home Address: _____

Home Phone: _____

Cell Phone: _____

Work Phone: _____

Email Address: _____

Notes: _____

_____

_____

_____

_____

_____

_____

_____

_____

ADDITIONAL FAMILY

First Name:_____

Last Name: _____

Maiden Name: _____

Date of Birth: _____

Home Address: _____

Home Phone: _____

Cell Phone: _____

Work Phone: _____

Email Address: _____

Notes: _____
_____
_____
_____
_____
_____
_____
_____
_____
_____
_____

First Name:_____

Last Name: _____

Maiden Name: _____

Date of Birth: _____

Home Address: _____

Home Phone: _____

Cell Phone: _____

Work Phone: _____

Email Address: _____

Notes: _____
_____
_____
_____
_____
_____
_____
_____
_____

ADDITIONAL FAMILY

First Name:_____

Last Name: _____

Maiden Name: _____

Date of Birth: _____

Home Address: _____

Home Phone: _____

Cell Phone: _____

Work Phone: _____

Email Address: _____

Notes: _____

_____

_____

_____

_____

_____

_____

_____

_____

_____

First Name:_____

Last Name: _____

Maiden Name: _____

Date of Birth: _____

Home Address: _____

Home Phone: _____

Cell Phone: _____

Work Phone: _____

Email Address: _____

Notes: _____

_____

_____

_____

_____

_____

_____

_____

_____

ADDITIONAL FAMILY

First Name:_____

Last Name: _____

Maiden Name: _____

Date of Birth: _____

Home Address: _____

Home Phone: _____

Cell Phone: _____

Work Phone: _____

Email Address: _____

Notes: _____

_____

_____

_____

_____

_____

_____

_____

_____

_____

_____

First Name:_____

Last Name: _____

Maiden Name: _____

Date of Birth: _____

Home Address: _____

Home Phone: _____

Cell Phone: _____

Work Phone: _____

Email Address: _____

Notes: _____

_____

_____

_____

_____

_____

_____

_____

_____

ADDITIONAL FAMILY

First Name:_____

Last Name: _____

Maiden Name: _____

Date of Birth: _____

Home Address: _____

Home Phone: _____

Cell Phone: _____

Work Phone: _____

Email Address: _____

Notes: _____
_____
_____
_____
_____
_____
_____
_____
_____
_____
_____
_____

First Name:_____

Last Name: _____

Maiden Name: _____

Date of Birth: _____

Home Address: _____

Home Phone: _____

Cell Phone: _____

Work Phone: _____

Email Address: _____

Notes: _____
_____
_____
_____
_____
_____
_____
_____
_____
_____

ADDITIONAL FAMILY

First Name:_____

Last Name: _____

Maiden Name: _____

Date of Birth: _____

Home Address: _____

Home Phone: _____

Cell Phone: _____

Work Phone: _____

Email Address: _____

Notes: _____
_____
_____
_____
_____
_____
_____
_____
_____
_____
_____
_____

First Name:_____

Last Name: _____

Maiden Name: _____

Date of Birth: _____

Home Address: _____

Home Phone: _____

Cell Phone: _____

Work Phone: _____

Email Address: _____

Notes: _____
_____
_____
_____
_____
_____
_____
_____
_____
_____
_____

ADDITIONAL FAMILY

First Name:_____

Last Name: _____

Maiden Name: _____

Date of Birth: _____

Home Address: _____

Home Phone: _____

Cell Phone: _____

Work Phone: _____

Email Address: _____

Notes: _____
_____
_____
_____
_____
_____
_____
_____
_____
_____
_____

First Name:_____

Last Name: _____

Maiden Name: _____

Date of Birth: _____

Home Address: _____

Home Phone: _____

Cell Phone: _____

Work Phone: _____

Email Address: _____

Notes: _____
_____
_____
_____
_____
_____
_____
_____
_____
_____

ADDITIONAL FAMILY

First Name:_____

Last Name: _____

Maiden Name: _____

Date of Birth: _____

Home Address: _____

Home Phone: _____

Cell Phone: _____

Work Phone: _____

Email Address: _____

Notes: _____
_____
_____
_____
_____
_____
_____
_____
_____
_____
_____

First Name:_____

Last Name: _____

Maiden Name: _____

Date of Birth: _____

Home Address: _____

Home Phone: _____

Cell Phone: _____

Work Phone: _____

Email Address: _____

Notes: _____
_____
_____
_____
_____
_____
_____
_____
_____

ADDITIONAL FAMILY

First Name:_____

Last Name: _____

Maiden Name: _____

Date of Birth: _____

Home Address: _____

Home Phone: _____

Cell Phone: _____

Work Phone: _____

Email Address: _____

Notes: _____
_____
_____
_____
_____
_____
_____
_____
_____
_____
_____

First Name:_____

Last Name: _____

Maiden Name: _____

Date of Birth: _____

Home Address: _____

Home Phone: _____

Cell Phone: _____

Work Phone: _____

Email Address: _____

Notes: _____
_____
_____
_____
_____
_____
_____
_____
_____

ADDITIONAL FAMILY

First Name:_____
Last Name: _____
Maiden Name: _____
Date of Birth: _____
Home Address: _____
Home Phone: _____
Cell Phone: _____
Work Phone: _____
Email Address: _____

Notes: _____
_____
_____
_____
_____
_____
_____
_____
_____
_____
_____

First Name:_____
Last Name: _____
Maiden Name: _____
Date of Birth: _____
Home Address: _____
Home Phone: _____
Cell Phone: _____
Work Phone: _____
Email Address: _____

Notes: _____
_____
_____
_____
_____
_____
_____
_____
_____
_____

ADDITIONAL FAMILY

First Name:_____

Last Name: _____

Maiden Name: _____

Date of Birth: _____

Home Address: _____

Home Phone: _____

Cell Phone: _____

Work Phone: _____

Email Address: _____

Notes: _____
_____
_____
_____
_____
_____
_____
_____
_____
_____
_____

First Name:_____

Last Name: _____

Maiden Name: _____

Date of Birth: _____

Home Address: _____

Home Phone: _____

Cell Phone: _____

Work Phone: _____

Email Address: _____

Notes: _____
_____
_____
_____
_____
_____
_____
_____
_____

ADDITIONAL FAMILY

First Name:_____

Last Name: _____

Maiden Name: _____

Date of Birth: _____

Home Address: _____

Home Phone: _____

Cell Phone: _____

Work Phone: _____

Email Address: _____

Notes: _____

_____

_____

_____

_____

_____

_____

_____

_____

_____

First Name:_____

Last Name: _____

Maiden Name: _____

Date of Birth: _____

Home Address: _____

Home Phone: _____

Cell Phone: _____

Work Phone: _____

Email Address: _____

Notes: _____

_____

_____

_____

_____

_____

_____

_____

_____

ADDITIONAL FAMILY

First Name:_____

Last Name: _____

Maiden Name: _____

Date of Birth: _____

Home Address: _____

Home Phone: _____

Cell Phone: _____

Work Phone: _____

Email Address: _____

Notes: _____
_____
_____
_____
_____
_____
_____
_____
_____
_____
_____

First Name:_____

Last Name: _____

Maiden Name: _____

Date of Birth: _____

Home Address: _____

Home Phone: _____

Cell Phone: _____

Work Phone: _____

Email Address: _____

Notes: _____
_____
_____
_____
_____
_____
_____
_____
_____
_____

MY FRIENDS

MY FRIENDS

First Name:_____

Last Name: _____

Maiden Name: _____

Date of Birth: _____

Home Address: _____

Home Phone: _____

Cell Phone: _____

Work Phone: _____

Email Address: _____

Notes: _____

_____

_____

_____

_____

_____

_____

_____

_____

_____

_____

First Name:_____

Last Name: _____

Maiden Name: _____

Date of Birth: _____

Home Address: _____

Home Phone: _____

Cell Phone: _____

Work Phone: _____

Email Address: _____

Notes: _____

_____

_____

_____

_____

_____

_____

_____

_____

_____

MY FRIENDS

First Name:_____

Last Name: _____

Maiden Name: _____

Date of Birth: _____

Home Address: _____

Home Phone: _____

Cell Phone: _____

Work Phone: _____

Email Address: _____

Notes: _____
_____
_____
_____
_____
_____
_____
_____
_____
_____
_____

First Name:_____

Last Name: _____

Maiden Name: _____

Date of Birth: _____

Home Address: _____

Home Phone: _____

Cell Phone: _____

Work Phone: _____

Email Address: _____

Notes: _____
_____
_____
_____
_____
_____
_____
_____
_____
_____

MY FRIENDS

First Name:_____

Last Name: _____

Maiden Name: _____

Date of Birth: _____

Home Address: _____

Home Phone: _____

Cell Phone: _____

Work Phone: _____

Email Address: _____

Notes: _____
_____
_____
_____
_____
_____
_____
_____
_____
_____
_____

First Name:_____

Last Name: _____

Maiden Name: _____

Date of Birth: _____

Home Address: _____

Home Phone: _____

Cell Phone: _____

Work Phone: _____

Email Address: _____

Notes: _____
_____
_____
_____
_____
_____
_____
_____
_____
_____

MY FRIENDS

First Name:_____

Last Name: _____

Maiden Name: _____

Date of Birth: _____

Home Address: _____

Home Phone: _____

Cell Phone: _____

Work Phone: _____

Email Address: _____

Notes: _____
_____
_____
_____
_____
_____
_____
_____
_____
_____
_____

First Name:_____

Last Name: _____

Maiden Name: _____

Date of Birth: _____

Home Address: _____

Home Phone: _____

Cell Phone: _____

Work Phone: _____

Email Address: _____

Notes: _____
_____
_____
_____
_____
_____
_____
_____
_____
_____

MY FRIENDS

First Name:_____

Last Name: _____

Maiden Name: _____

Date of Birth: _____

Home Address: _____

Home Phone: _____

Cell Phone: _____

Work Phone: _____

Email Address: _____

Notes: _____
_____
_____
_____
_____
_____
_____
_____
_____
_____

First Name:_____

Last Name: _____

Maiden Name: _____

Date of Birth: _____

Home Address: _____

Home Phone: _____

Cell Phone: _____

Work Phone: _____

Email Address: _____

Notes: _____
_____
_____
_____
_____
_____
_____
_____
_____

MY FRIENDS

First Name:_____

Last Name: _____

Maiden Name: _____

Date of Birth: _____

Home Address: _____

Home Phone: _____

Cell Phone: _____

Work Phone: _____

Email Address: _____

Notes: _____
_____
_____
_____
_____
_____
_____
_____
_____
_____
_____

First Name:_____

Last Name: _____

Maiden Name: _____

Date of Birth: _____

Home Address: _____

Home Phone: _____

Cell Phone: _____

Work Phone: _____

Email Address: _____

Notes: _____
_____
_____
_____
_____
_____
_____
_____
_____
_____

MY FRIENDS

First Name:_____
Last Name: _____
Maiden Name: _____
Date of Birth: _____
Home Address: _____
Home Phone: _____
Cell Phone: _____
Work Phone: _____
Email Address: _____

Notes: _____
_____
_____
_____
_____
_____
_____
_____
_____
_____
_____

First Name:_____
Last Name: _____
Maiden Name: _____
Date of Birth: _____
Home Address: _____
Home Phone: _____
Cell Phone: _____
Work Phone: _____
Email Address: _____

Notes: _____
_____
_____
_____
_____
_____
_____
_____
_____
_____

MY FRIENDS

First Name:_____

Last Name: _____

Maiden Name: _____

Date of Birth: _____

Home Address: _____

Home Phone: _____

Cell Phone: _____

Work Phone: _____

Email Address: _____

Notes: _____
_____
_____
_____
_____
_____
_____
_____
_____
_____
_____

First Name:_____

Last Name: _____

Maiden Name: _____

Date of Birth: _____

Home Address: _____

Home Phone: _____

Cell Phone: _____

Work Phone: _____

Email Address: _____

Notes: _____
_____
_____
_____
_____
_____
_____
_____
_____
_____
_____

MY FRIENDS

First Name:_____

Last Name: _____

Maiden Name: _____

Date of Birth: _____

Home Address: _____

Home Phone: _____

Cell Phone: _____

Work Phone: _____

Email Address: _____

Notes: _____
_____
_____
_____
_____
_____
_____
_____
_____
_____
_____

First Name:_____

Last Name: _____

Maiden Name: _____

Date of Birth: _____

Home Address: _____

Home Phone: _____

Cell Phone: _____

Work Phone: _____

Email Address: _____

Notes: _____
_____
_____
_____
_____
_____
_____
_____
_____
_____

MY FRIENDS

First Name:_____

Last Name: _____

Maiden Name: _____

Date of Birth: _____

Home Address: _____

Home Phone: _____

Cell Phone: _____

Work Phone: _____

Email Address: _____

Notes: _____
_____
_____
_____
_____
_____
_____
_____
_____
_____
_____

First Name:_____

Last Name: _____

Maiden Name: _____

Date of Birth: _____

Home Address: _____

Home Phone: _____

Cell Phone: _____

Work Phone: _____

Email Address: _____

Notes: _____
_____
_____
_____
_____
_____
_____
_____
_____

MY FRIENDS

First Name:_____

Last Name: _____

Maiden Name: _____

Date of Birth: _____

Home Address: _____

Home Phone: _____

Cell Phone: _____

Work Phone: _____

Email Address: _____

Notes: _____

_____

_____

_____

_____

_____

_____

_____

_____

_____

First Name:_____

Last Name: _____

Maiden Name: _____

Date of Birth: _____

Home Address: _____

Home Phone: _____

Cell Phone: _____

Work Phone: _____

Email Address: _____

Notes: _____

_____

_____

_____

_____

_____

_____

_____

_____

MY FRIENDS

First Name:_____
Last Name: _____
Maiden Name: _____
Date of Birth: _____
Home Address: _____
Home Phone: _____
Cell Phone: _____
Work Phone: _____
Email Address: _____

Notes: _____
_____
_____
_____
_____
_____
_____
_____
_____
_____
_____

First Name:_____
Last Name: _____
Maiden Name: _____
Date of Birth: _____
Home Address: _____
Home Phone: _____
Cell Phone: _____
Work Phone: _____
Email Address: _____

Notes: _____
_____
_____
_____
_____
_____
_____
_____
_____
_____

MY FRIENDS

First Name:_____
Last Name: _____
Maiden Name: _____
Date of Birth: _____
Home Address: _____
Home Phone: _____
Cell Phone: _____
Work Phone: _____
Email Address: _____

Notes: _____
_____
_____
_____
_____
_____
_____
_____
_____
_____

First Name:_____
Last Name: _____
Maiden Name: _____
Date of Birth: _____
Home Address: _____
Home Phone: _____
Cell Phone: _____
Work Phone: _____
Email Address: _____

Notes: _____
_____
_____
_____
_____
_____
_____
_____
_____

MY FRIENDS

First Name:_____

Last Name: _____

Maiden Name: _____

Date of Birth: _____

Home Address: _____

Home Phone: _____

Cell Phone: _____

Work Phone: _____

Email Address: _____

Notes: _____
_____
_____
_____
_____
_____
_____
_____
_____
_____
_____

First Name:_____

Last Name: _____

Maiden Name: _____

Date of Birth: _____

Home Address: _____

Home Phone: _____

Cell Phone: _____

Work Phone: _____

Email Address: _____

Notes: _____
_____
_____
_____
_____
_____
_____
_____
_____
_____

MY FRIENDS

First Name:_____
Last Name: _____
Maiden Name: _____
Date of Birth: _____
Home Address: _____
Home Phone: _____
Cell Phone: _____
Work Phone: _____
Email Address: _____

Notes: _____
_____
_____
_____
_____
_____
_____
_____
_____
_____
_____

First Name:_____
Last Name: _____
Maiden Name: _____
Date of Birth: _____
Home Address: _____
Home Phone: _____
Cell Phone: _____
Work Phone: _____
Email Address: _____

Notes: _____
_____
_____
_____
_____
_____
_____
_____
_____

MY FRIENDS

First Name:_____

Last Name: _____

Maiden Name: _____

Date of Birth: _____

Home Address: _____

Home Phone: _____

Cell Phone: _____

Work Phone: _____

Email Address: _____

Notes: _____
_____
_____
_____
_____
_____
_____
_____
_____
_____
_____

First Name:_____

Last Name: _____

Maiden Name: _____

Date of Birth: _____

Home Address: _____

Home Phone: _____

Cell Phone: _____

Work Phone: _____

Email Address: _____

Notes: _____
_____
_____
_____
_____
_____
_____
_____
_____

MY FRIENDS

First Name:_____

Last Name: _____

Maiden Name: _____

Date of Birth: _____

Home Address: _____

Home Phone: _____

Cell Phone: _____

Work Phone: _____

Email Address: _____

Notes: _____
_____
_____
_____
_____
_____
_____
_____
_____
_____
_____

First Name:_____

Last Name: _____

Maiden Name: _____

Date of Birth: _____

Home Address: _____

Home Phone: _____

Cell Phone: _____

Work Phone: _____

Email Address: _____

Notes: _____
_____
_____
_____
_____
_____
_____
_____
_____
_____

MY FRIENDS

First Name:_____
Last Name: _____
Maiden Name: _____
Date of Birth: _____
Home Address: _____
Home Phone: _____
Cell Phone: _____
Work Phone: _____
Email Address: _____

Notes: _____
_____
_____
_____
_____
_____
_____
_____
_____
_____

First Name:_____
Last Name: _____
Maiden Name: _____
Date of Birth: _____
Home Address: _____
Home Phone: _____
Cell Phone: _____
Work Phone: _____
Email Address: _____

Notes: _____
_____
_____
_____
_____
_____
_____
_____
_____

MY FRIENDS

First Name:_____

Last Name: _____

Maiden Name: _____

Date of Birth: _____

Home Address: _____

Home Phone: _____

Cell Phone: _____

Work Phone: _____

Email Address: _____

Notes: _____
_____
_____
_____
_____
_____
_____
_____
_____
_____
_____

First Name:_____

Last Name: _____

Maiden Name: _____

Date of Birth: _____

Home Address: _____

Home Phone: _____

Cell Phone: _____

Work Phone: _____

Email Address: _____

Notes: _____
_____
_____
_____
_____
_____
_____
_____
_____
_____

MY FRIENDS

First Name:_____

Last Name: _____

Maiden Name: _____

Date of Birth: _____

Home Address: _____

Home Phone: _____

Cell Phone: _____

Work Phone: _____

Email Address: _____

Notes: _____

_____

_____

_____

_____

_____

_____

_____

_____

_____

First Name:_____

Last Name: _____

Maiden Name: _____

Date of Birth: _____

Home Address: _____

Home Phone: _____

Cell Phone: _____

Work Phone: _____

Email Address: _____

Notes: _____

_____

_____

_____

_____

_____

_____

_____

_____

_____

MY FRIENDS

First Name:_____

Last Name: _____

Maiden Name: _____

Date of Birth: _____

Home Address: _____

Home Phone: _____

Cell Phone: _____

Work Phone: _____

Email Address: _____

Notes: _____

_____

_____

_____

_____

_____

_____

_____

_____

_____

First Name:_____

Last Name: _____

Maiden Name: _____

Date of Birth: _____

Home Address: _____

Home Phone: _____

Cell Phone: _____

Work Phone: _____

Email Address: _____

Notes: _____

_____

_____

_____

_____

_____

_____

_____

_____

MY FRIENDS

First Name:_____

Last Name: _____

Maiden Name: _____

Date of Birth: _____

Home Address: _____

Home Phone: _____

Cell Phone: _____

Work Phone: _____

Email Address: _____

Notes: _____

_____

_____

_____

_____

_____

_____

_____

_____

_____

First Name:_____

Last Name: _____

Maiden Name: _____

Date of Birth: _____

Home Address: _____

Home Phone: _____

Cell Phone: _____

Work Phone: _____

Email Address: _____

Notes: _____

_____

_____

_____

_____

_____

_____

_____

_____

MY FRIENDS

First Name:_____

Last Name: _____

Maiden Name: _____

Date of Birth: _____

Home Address: _____

Home Phone: _____

Cell Phone: _____

Work Phone: _____

Email Address: _____

Notes: _____

_____

_____

_____

_____

_____

_____

_____

_____

_____

First Name:_____

Last Name: _____

Maiden Name: _____

Date of Birth: _____

Home Address: _____

Home Phone: _____

Cell Phone: _____

Work Phone: _____

Email Address: _____

Notes: _____

_____

_____

_____

_____

_____

_____

_____

_____

MY FRIENDS

First Name:_____

Last Name: _____

Maiden Name: _____

Date of Birth: _____

Home Address: _____

Home Phone: _____

Cell Phone: _____

Work Phone: _____

Email Address: _____

Notes: _____
_____
_____
_____
_____
_____
_____
_____
_____
_____
_____

First Name:_____

Last Name: _____

Maiden Name: _____

Date of Birth: _____

Home Address: _____

Home Phone: _____

Cell Phone: _____

Work Phone: _____

Email Address: _____

Notes: _____
_____
_____
_____
_____
_____
_____
_____
_____
_____

Extra Entries

_____

First Name:_____
Last Name: _____
Maiden Name: _____
Date of Birth: _____
Home Address: _____
Home Phone: _____
Cell Phone: _____
Work Phone: _____
Email Address: _____

Notes: _____
_____
_____
_____
_____
_____
_____
_____
_____
_____
_____

First Name:_____
Last Name: _____
Maiden Name: _____
Date of Birth: _____
Home Address: _____
Home Phone: _____
Cell Phone: _____
Work Phone: _____
Email Address: _____

Notes: _____
_____
_____
_____
_____
_____
_____
_____
_____
_____

First Name:_____

Last Name: _____

Maiden Name: _____

Date of Birth: _____

Home Address: _____

Home Phone: _____

Cell Phone: _____

Work Phone: _____

Email Address: _____

Notes: _____
_____
_____
_____
_____
_____
_____
_____
_____
_____
_____

First Name:_____

Last Name: _____

Maiden Name: _____

Date of Birth: _____

Home Address: _____

Home Phone: _____

Cell Phone: _____

Work Phone: _____

Email Address: _____

Notes: _____
_____
_____
_____
_____
_____
_____
_____
_____

_____

First Name:_____

Last Name: _____

Maiden Name: _____

Date of Birth: _____

Home Address: _____

Home Phone: _____

Cell Phone: _____

Work Phone: _____

Email Address: _____

Notes: _____

_____

_____

_____

_____

_____

_____

_____

_____

_____

_____

First Name:_____

Last Name: _____

Maiden Name: _____

Date of Birth: _____

Home Address: _____

Home Phone: _____

Cell Phone: _____

Work Phone: _____

Email Address: _____

Notes: _____

_____

_____

_____

_____

_____

_____

_____

_____

_____

First Name:_____
Last Name: _____
Maiden Name: _____
Date of Birth: _____
Home Address: _____
Home Phone: _____
Cell Phone: _____
Work Phone: _____
Email Address: _____

Notes: _____
_____
_____
_____
_____
_____
_____
_____
_____
_____

First Name:_____
Last Name: _____
Maiden Name: _____
Date of Birth: _____
Home Address: _____
Home Phone: _____
Cell Phone: _____
Work Phone: _____
Email Address: _____

Notes: _____
_____
_____
_____
_____
_____
_____
_____
_____

_____

First Name:_____
Last Name: _____
Maiden Name: _____
Date of Birth: _____
Home Address: _____
Home Phone: _____
Cell Phone: _____
Work Phone: _____
Email Address: _____

Notes: _____
_____
_____
_____
_____
_____
_____
_____
_____
_____

First Name:_____
Last Name: _____
Maiden Name: _____
Date of Birth: _____
Home Address: _____
Home Phone: _____
Cell Phone: _____
Work Phone: _____
Email Address: _____

Notes: _____
_____
_____
_____
_____
_____
_____
_____
_____
_____

_____

First Name:_____
Last Name: _____
Maiden Name: _____
Date of Birth: _____
Home Address: _____
Home Phone: _____
Cell Phone: _____
Work Phone: _____
Email Address: _____

Notes: _____
_____
_____
_____
_____
_____
_____
_____
_____
_____
_____
_____

First Name:_____
Last Name: _____
Maiden Name: _____
Date of Birth: _____
Home Address: _____
Home Phone: _____
Cell Phone: _____
Work Phone: _____
Email Address: _____

Notes: _____
_____
_____
_____
_____
_____
_____
_____
_____
_____

_____

First Name:_____

Last Name: _____

Maiden Name: _____

Date of Birth: _____

Home Address: _____

Home Phone: _____

Cell Phone: _____

Work Phone: _____

Email Address: _____

Notes: _____

_____

_____

_____

_____

_____

_____

_____

_____

_____

_____

First Name:_____

Last Name: _____

Maiden Name: _____

Date of Birth: _____

Home Address: _____

Home Phone: _____

Cell Phone: _____

Work Phone: _____

Email Address: _____

Notes: _____

_____

_____

_____

_____

_____

_____

_____

_____

_____

_____

First Name:_____

Last Name: _____

Maiden Name: _____

Date of Birth: _____

Home Address: _____

Home Phone: _____

Cell Phone: _____

Work Phone: _____

Email Address: _____

Notes: _____
_____
_____
_____
_____
_____
_____
_____
_____
_____
_____

First Name:_____

Last Name: _____

Maiden Name: _____

Date of Birth: _____

Home Address: _____

Home Phone: _____

Cell Phone: _____

Work Phone: _____

Email Address: _____

Notes: _____
_____
_____
_____
_____
_____
_____
_____
_____

_____

First Name:_____
Last Name: _____
Maiden Name: _____
Date of Birth: _____
Home Address: _____
Home Phone: _____
Cell Phone: _____
Work Phone: _____
Email Address: _____

Notes: _____
_____
_____
_____
_____
_____
_____
_____
_____
_____
_____

First Name:_____
Last Name: _____
Maiden Name: _____
Date of Birth: _____
Home Address: _____
Home Phone: _____
Cell Phone: _____
Work Phone: _____
Email Address: _____

Notes: _____
_____
_____
_____
_____
_____
_____
_____
_____
_____

_____

First Name:_____

Last Name: _____

Maiden Name: _____

Date of Birth: _____

Home Address: _____

Home Phone: _____

Cell Phone: _____

Work Phone: _____

Email Address: _____

Notes: _____

_____

_____

_____

_____

_____

_____

_____

_____

_____

_____

First Name:_____

Last Name: _____

Maiden Name: _____

Date of Birth: _____

Home Address: _____

Home Phone: _____

Cell Phone: _____

Work Phone: _____

Email Address: _____

Notes: _____

_____

_____

_____

_____

_____

_____

_____

_____

_____

_____

First Name:_____

Last Name: _____

Maiden Name: _____

Date of Birth: _____

Home Address: _____

Home Phone: _____

Cell Phone: _____

Work Phone: _____

Email Address: _____

Notes: _____

_____

_____

_____

_____

_____

_____

_____

_____

_____

First Name:_____

Last Name: _____

Maiden Name: _____

Date of Birth: _____

Home Address: _____

Home Phone: _____

Cell Phone: _____

Work Phone: _____

Email Address: _____

Notes: _____

_____

_____

_____

_____

_____

_____

_____

_____

_____

First Name:_____
Last Name: _____
Maiden Name: _____
Date of Birth: _____
Home Address: _____
Home Phone: _____
Cell Phone: _____
Work Phone: _____
Email Address: _____

Notes: _____
_____
_____
_____
_____
_____
_____
_____
_____
_____

First Name:_____
Last Name: _____
Maiden Name: _____
Date of Birth: _____
Home Address: _____
Home Phone: _____
Cell Phone: _____
Work Phone: _____
Email Address: _____

Notes: _____
_____
_____
_____
_____
_____
_____
_____
_____

Notes: _____

Notes: _____

Notes: _____

www.ingramcontent.com/pod-product-compliance
Lightning Source LLC
Chambersburg PA
CBHW081220020426

42331CB00012B/3061